ACTIVATORS

BASKETBALL

Clive Gifford

Illustrated by Bert Jackson

Consultant: Norman Waldron,
English Schools Basketball Association

D1586033

*Hodder
Children's
Books*

a division of Hodder Headline plc

The author would like to thank his wife, Jane, who played representative basketball for her home-state of Queensland in Australia, and to the crew at Hodder, especially Anne Clark and Lyn Coutts, for making this play happen. A special thanks to Mr Compton (Clive's first and best basketball coach) who put in hours of extra coaching help and put up with Clive.

Text copyright 1999 © Clive Gifford
Illustrations copyright 1999 © Bert Jackson
Published by Hodder Children's Books 1999

'ACTIVATOR' is a registered trade mark owned by and used with the permission of Addison Wesley Longman Limited.

Edited by Lyn Coutts
Consultant: Norman Waldron, English Schools Basketball Association
Designed by Fiona Webb
Series designed by Fiona Webb

The right of Clive Gifford and Bert Jackson to be identified as the author and illustrator of the work has been asserted by them in accordance with the Copyright, Designs and Patents Act 1988.

10 9 8 7 6 5 4 3 2 1

A catalogue record for this book is available from the British Library.

ISBN: 0 340 736305

Printed by Clays Ltd, St Ives plc

Hodder Children's Books
a division of Hodder Headline plc
338 Euston Road
London NW1 3BH

Meet the author

It all started so well for Clive. Tall beyond his years, he relied on his height (Well, have you ever seen a 6ft-tall nine year old?) to attack and defend. Because of this natural advantage Clive never put much thought into his game until the day that he realised that everyone else was suddenly taller than him.

Forced into having a big think about his basketball future and inspired by several bespectacled NBA players – far too ancient for you to have heard of – Clive worked at improving his game and became captain of his school side. Another couple of centimetres taller and he could have grabbed a top slot at club level.

Clive still likes to lumber round the court sinking the odd lay-up and occasional three-pointer, even though fast breaks and slam dunks are beyond him now. In fact, officials sometimes call double-teaming when he's marking, such is the size of his frame squeezed into an XXXXXL replica NBA top.

Introduction

Yes! Yes! Yes! I've been given the chance to write this book and I'm so excited. Why? Because basketball is a fabulous sport. The Americans know it (Their NBA players are among the country's most famous sportsmen and woman.). Most European countries know it, and even Australia has latched onto basketball fever. And it won't be long before basketball makes it big-time in Britain.

Basketball is an awesome game, incredible to play, exciting to watch and low on injuries. As an athletic adventure, it's great exercise for body and mind. One moment you can be sprinting across court, the next aiming to shoot with ice-cold accuracy and all the while your brain is working on strategies to outwit your opponents. Fantastic!

If you're still not convinced why I and millions of others are so nuts about the game, listen up. Forget 0-0 score draw games (boring), basketball is big on points with 100 scoring shots likely in a game. Imagine how you would feel if you made 10 or 15 of these. Top of the world or what?

To get a piece of the basketball action, all you have to do is read this book, practise the drills and plays and get a team together. One day you could be slam-dunking your way into basketball history.

Contents

Introduction   iv

1 Basketball basics   2

2 Getting started   16

3 Court craft   30

4 Dribbling and lay-ups   42

5 Shooting   56

6 Defending and rebounding   70

7 Attacking skills and tactics   82

8 Brain over ball   96

9 Hoop dreams   103

   Want to know more?   112

   Glossary   119

   Index   121

Basketball basics

With its small court, all-action fast moves and high-scoring games, basketball is exhilarating to watch, but even better to play. Anyone who has ever scored a long-range shot or has run the length of the court to stuff a shot through the hoop knows what a great sensation it is. It's up there with the very best moments in any sport – golf's hole-in-one, a great try in rugby, a hat-trick of goals in soccer, and ace serves in tennis. The difference with basketball is that, with hard work and practice, you can experience great moments not just once in a season or a career, but more than once in every game!

Next time you or a friend is abducted by aliens, ask them what sport in the solar system their galactic money is on. Bet they answer, basketball.

A peach of a game

Basketball was invented in 1891 by Dr. James Naismith, a teacher in Massachusetts, USA. His students were bored in the gym during winter so Naismith invented a game where a football was thrown into peach baskets hung from balconies around the gym. The fact that a stepladder was needed to retrieve the ball each time a player scored didn't stop 'basket-ball' going down a real treat with his students.

Dream play

It's a big game, your team's a point down and there's seconds left on the clock. Your team have the ball, but you're heavily marked. It's the same guy who's been on you all game and he's good, but he still falls for your favourite fake. You get clear, take a crisp pass and face the basket. It's now or never. You shoot just before the buzzer goes and everyone watches as the ball sails through the air. Will it? Won't it? It does! You score, your team win and frankly, sport just doesn't get better than that.

Fab five

Basketball is the business. Once played, you'll be hooked. Here are five reasons to get into basketball:

1 It's fast-moving and exciting.
2 Every player is constantly involved in the play, passing shooting, dribbling and defending.
3 It's high-scoring with every player having an almost equal chance of shooting and scoring.
4 It costs so little to play.
5 It's a cool game – so cool, it hurts!

In court

Basketball is a five-a-side game played on a rectangular court. Hoops are fixed to posts at either end and the object of the game is to score points by throwing a ball so that it goes through the hoop from above. Two points are given for a basket in open play, three points are awarded if

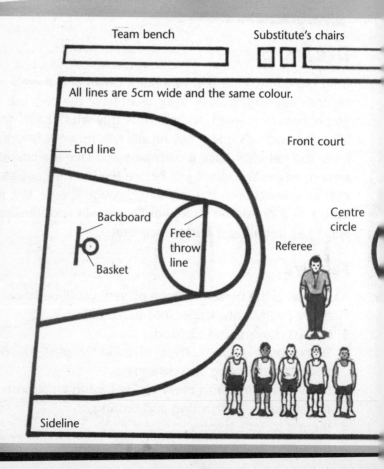

Team bench

Substitute's chairs

All lines are 5cm wide and the same colour.

End line

Front court

Backboard

Free-throw line

Basket

Centre circle

Referee

Sideline

the shot has taken place from behind the three-point line marked on the court. When a player is fouled, he or she may be awarded free throws, each of which are worth a point. The team with the most points at the end of the second half wins.

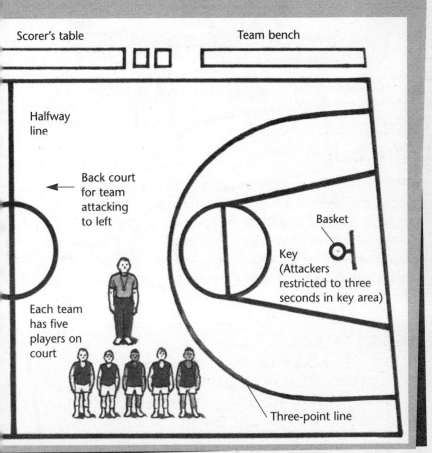

Scorer's table

Team bench

Halfway line

Back court for team attacking to left

Basket

Key
(Attackers restricted to three seconds in key area)

Each team has five players on court

Three-point line

The hoop

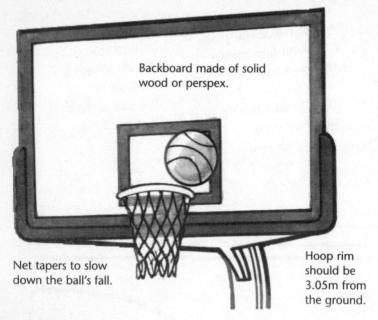

Backboard made of solid wood or perspex.

Net tapers to slow down the ball's fall.

Hoop rim should be 3.05m from the ground.

The ball

Slightly larger than a soccer ball and heavier at around 650g, a basketball has a grainy surface that makes it easier to hold. The ball should be pumped up so that when dropped (not pushed) from a height of 1.8m, it bounces to about waist height (1.2-1.4m). To keep the ball well-inflated, inflate it with a bicycle-tyre pump. You can buy adaptors that will connect the pump to the ball.

Olympic event

Basketball exploded into popularity and in 1936 – just 45 years after Naismith invented it – basketball became an Olympic sport. The gold medals were presented to the winning team by none less than Naismith himself.

Don't fear the gear

Basketball courts cost big cash; playing gear doesn't, or more accurately, shouldn't. Sportswear companies try their hardest to convince you that unless you wear their branded kit, you'll be a loser with a capital 'L'. Rubbish!

Without realising it, you've probably got all the basketball gear you'll ever need: good trainers, socks, vest or T-shirt and a pair of shorts. Loose fitting shorts and vest or T-shirt are the in-thing for basketball and have been for years. Don't wear a shirt with a zip or buttons as they may catch on someone's face. For warming up in a cold gym or outside, a tracksuit is a good idea. Otherwise, it's up to you.

Dressed for success. Towelling bands on wrists and head help mop up the sweat. Don't wear a watch or any type of jewellery, and check that trainer laces are tied securely and not trailing on the ground.

Avoid the fashion trap

1 Buy a regular vest and shorts that are dead comfortable, cheap and hard-wearing.

2 Get your hands on a cheap Chicago Bulls vest in a seconds or reject sale. Make it authentic with a tear here and there and then pretend that it was once worn by rough, tough Dennis Rodman.

3 Buy a cheap basketball vest that has some weird name or logo on it. When friends ask what the name or logo stands for, tell them it's a top American college team.

Rubber sole

Low cut shoe

High ankle
support boot

The stresses on your feet and ankles caused by twisting, turning and jumping during a hectic game are large, so good shoes that have been properly fitted are important. There are two basic types, the basketball boot with high ankle support and the lower-cut shoe. To get a good grip on the smooth court surface, shoes should have smoothish rubber sole – deep tread trainers are best on grass.

Getting the right shoes

1 Try to simulate playing conditions. Shop late in the day when your feet are swollen and wear the same type or numbers of pairs of socks as you would in a game.

2 Lace the shoes tightly. Are they a comfortable fit all over?

3 Check for good padding, especially around the ankles.

4 Make quick starts and stops in the shoe shop, do the trainers perform for you?

Sock it to me

Many players opt for a slightly bigger than normal trainer that they fill by wearing two pairs of socks. This extra padding does help prevent blisters. Whether you wear one or two pairs, cotton towelling socks get the thumbs up.

Shock stoppers

Shock-absorbing insoles (Sorbothane are one highly-recommended brand) can be a big help. These provide lots of cushioning particularly for the ball and heel of your foot – the key contact areas.

Basketball shoes and boots tend to wear out from the inside (particularly if you play indoors). This can leave you with a boot that looks okay on the outside, but has no internal padding for your feet. Fitting a shock-absorbing insole can extend the life of the shoe.

Rules, rules, rules

It took Dr. Naismith just an hour to draw up the first set of basketball rules. But as the game has evolved and progressed over the years, the rules have been become longer and longer. In this book, you'll become familiar with the main rules that will affect your game. If you're really eager to know more, you can buy a full set of rules (see page 117) or ask your coach to lend you a set.

One rule for some ...

The rules shown throughout this book are the ones you'll play under. They're run by the international organisation FIBA, whereas the pro players in the NBA use a slightly different set. On page 108 there's a summary of the key differences between the NBA and FIBA.

"Jump ball"

"Cancel score"

Here are two of the referee's hand signals. You'll find more throughout the book.

Playing time and officials

Games are split into two 20-minute halves (or four quarters of 12 minutes in the NBA). If the score is a draw at the end of full time, five-minute periods of overtime are played out to find a winner.

Each new period of play is started with a jump ball between a player from each side, and ends with the referee's whistle. There's usually two refs. They signal fouls, violations and other stoppages with their whistle and hand signals. Additional officials can include a timer, a scorekeeper and a shot clock operator.

Stop the clock!

Stoppages

Play continues until the ball goes out the side or back of the court (out-of bounds), a time-out is called by one team or the referee blows for a foul or violation. Whenever the referee's whistle blows, the game stops and so does the game clock. The game and game clock only re-start when the last free throw of a series is taken or from a throw-in when the ball is touched by the first on-court player.

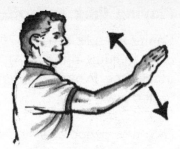

Time

Violation – Out of Bounds

Substitutions and time-outs

A team can have up to five substitutes. Rolling substitutions, which means a player can leave and re-enter the game as many times as the coach likes, are allowed during a stoppage. Each team is allowed a total of five one-minute breaks called charged time-outs. Coaches use these to change tactics. Other time-outs can be called by the referee if there is a serious injury. In all cases, the game clock stops.

Re-setting the shot clock

Official's time-out

Charged time-out

Substitution

Three vital time rules

1 A team has 30 seconds (24 seconds in the NBA) to make a shot on the basket. If they fail to do so in that time, the ball passes to the other team.

2 A team in possession in their defensive half, must cross the halfway line within ten seconds or the ball goes to the other team.

3 When the defending side has the ball, no attacker can remain in the key-shaped area for more than three seconds. Defenders can stay in for as long as they like.

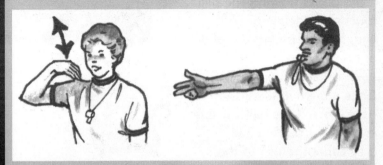

Timed-out   *Three-second rule infraction*

Travelling and other no-no's

The ball is moved around the court by passing to team-mates or by moving and bouncing the ball (dribbling). Dribbling can be with either hand, but never with both. Once a player has stopped dribbling and is holding the ball, he cannot start dribbling again. This is called a double dribble. A player cannot kick or punch the ball. He also can't hold the ball and run with it. This is called travelling.

If the player holding the ball touches a sideline or end line, the ball is considered out of bounds and the other team is handed possession. Once a team in possession have crossed the halfway line into their attacking half, they cannot return to the back court without giving up possession to the other team.

Ball returned to back of court

Illegal dribble   *Travelling*

Two points   *Three points*

Scoring and interference

When one team scores a basket (or the last free throw), possession switches and the other team restarts the game from the end line. The referee signals to the scorer how many points have been scored.

A shot can be blocked as it leaves the hand of the shooter, but the ball and the basket must not be interfered with as the ball travels down towards the hoop. If the defence interfere in this way, two points are awarded against them. If the attack interfere, possession is passed to the defending team and no points are awarded if the shot goes in.

That's enough rules for the moment, let's get playing!

2 Getting started

Sentenced to a long stretch

Now, you're itching to play, but first take five or so minutes out to loosen up and stretch. Stretching and warming up are vital for top performance and for preventing injuries. If it's good enough for Hakeem, The Shaq, Kobe and all the other top pros to stretch and warm up big time, then it's certainly good enough for you.

Warming up can be fun if you perform sets of passing and running drills with friends. You'll find plenty of these dotted throughout the book. For a full routine of stretches, get the low-down from your gym teacher or basketball coach. If neither are available, watch an experienced basketball player go through their routine. Whatever routine you get into, make sure your legs and body are fully stretched.

Warming up

You can warm yourself up without a basketball. This pair of players are performing star jumps.

This player is carefully stretching his hamstring muscles under the eye of his coach.

These three players are performing fast-moving dribbling and passing practice moves around the court.

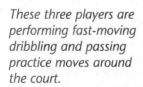

A bit of shooting practice in a varied warm-up routine never hurt anyone.

Catching

Ever dropped or fumbled a good, clean pass? Of course you have – everyone does from time to time. Chances are it happened because of one of these three situations below:

Your eyes didn't follow the ball right into your hands. A ball can dip down as it loses speed. Many people look away at the last moment, sizing up their next move. A catch isn't over until you have full control of the ball.

Your body wasn't balanced (see balanced stance below) and your arms weren't spread correctly to receive the catch. Use both hands to catch the ball where you can.

Catching the ball with your hands rigid and locked at the wrists, causes the ball to bounce out. To play with 'soft' hands, bring your hands back and in a little as the ball lands. This cushions the ball on impact.

Balanced stance

A good balanced stance with your body – and mind – prepared for a catch is what you want to achieve. See how this player's feet are apart and his head is up. His hands and arms are ready for a catch.

Stopping and pivoting

Once the basketball is in your hands, you can't move with it unless you're dribbling. Players new to basketball often stand frozen on the spot holding the ball, they forget that they can turn to the left or right, providing one foot, the pivot foot, remains planted in the same place.

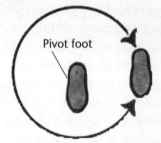

Pivot foot

With the pivot foot staying in one position, you can repeatedly move your other foot in any direction.

Pivoting is such a handy skill. It makes me cry to think that you wouldn't use it properly. After all, it requires little athleticism or brainpower. Yet, it allows you to see and potentially pass in any direction and can help keep you clear of a defender's attentions.

Clock game drill

Get as many players as possible to stand in a circle, about three to five metres away from you standing in the middle. Players call their name or their position on the clock, and you pivot round so that your body is facing them before throwing an accurate chest pass.

On the move

If you're moving when you catch the ball, you've got to stop and pivot within two steps otherwise a travelling violation will be called. When you land with both feet on the floor at the same time (a jump stop), you can choose which is your pivot foot. When you catch the ball in mid-air, make the first foot that lands your pivot foot. Bring your second foot forward in a normal running motion. It should land ahead of your pivot foot to balance you as you stop.

Stride stop

STEP 1 ▲
Catch the ball whilst on the move.

STEP 2 ▲
Land on your pivot foot while your other leg follows through.

◄ **STEP 3**
You're now in a balanced stance position and ready for action.

Pass class

Let's look at the triple-threat stance and your first basic play, the chest pass.

Triple-threat stance

When you have the ball, try to start with this stance which will worry a defender. Why? Because standing like this, you pose three different threats. You can pass, shoot or dribble easily from this position. The defender will know this and as a result, his movements may be uncertain.

In the triple-threat stance your feet are shoulder width apart. Your head is up and the ball is held firmly and close at around chest level.

Chest pass

The basic pass is called the chest pass because it is made from the chest. The idea is that as your arms push out forwards, the ball should zip horizontally to the receiver. Use the chest pass for close and medium-range passing. As you'll be making more chest passes per game than any other, it's something you've just got to get right.

CHEST PASS

STEP 1 ▶

Adopt the triple-threat stance and hold the ball with your fingers, not your palms. Thumbs are behind the ball and your wrists flexed backwards.

◀ STEP 2

Make the pass by pushing your arms out sharply and moving your body in the direction you're making the pass. Keep your eyes on the receiver.

STEP 3 ▶

As your arms straighten, flick your wrists forwards to release the ball. Your hands follow-through, pointing in the direction of the pass.

Chest pass checklist

1 Use for passes under five or six metres.

2 The ball should travel perfectly horizontal to the receiver.

3 Once you've decided to make a pass, make it quickly.

4 Don't make the pass if there's a defender in the way.

Overhead pass

This is a little like a chest pass, but with arms raised above your head. Hold the ball above and just in front of your head. Keep your eyes on your target and step forward in to the throw. As you do so, release the ball with a snap of your wrists. It's the wrists and lower arms that provide the power for the overhead pass.

STEP 1 **STEP 2**

The overhead pass is great as an outlet pass or as a short pass over a close defender. If you take too long and your play is obvious, the defender may block it.

Pass and catch drill

Stand one or two long paces from a wall and chest pass the ball vigorously. To sharpen your skills, aim the ball a couple of centimetres to either side of your mark, so that the ball comes back at a slightly different angle each time.

Overhead and chest pass drill

You and a friend stand three to five metres apart and exchange chest and overhead passes. Once you've got those down, start on an end line of the court, the width of the key apart, and move up and down the court swapping passes.

Bounce passes

I love bounce passes. It amazes me the number of times you can successfully get this pass out when other options fail. Novice basketball players especially are fooled by this pass, but only if you do it right.

Two-handed bounce pass

This is the simple version and only works when the passing lane is clear or when the defender is standing some way away from you. It's a lot like a chest pass, but angled down so that it strikes the floor about two-thirds of the way towards the receiver.

STEP 1 ▶

Begin in the triple-threat stance with the ball gathered in and your hands gripping the back and sides of the ball. Keep the thumbs pointing up and maintain easy control of the ball.

STEP 2 ▶

Start extending your arms out and downwards, aiming the ball towards the floor ahead where you intend the ball to bounce. A bounce-point about two-thirds of the way to the receiver is about right.

◀ STEP 3

Extend your arms as you project the ball away from you. Complete the pass and don't dawdle. If you hang onto the ball, you're giving defenders a clear idea of what you intend doing. This is called telegraphing a pass.

STEP 4 ▶

As in the chest pass, your arms straighten on the follow through. As you complete the pass, the backs of your hands should be facing inwards. The ball should bounce off the floor to be caught by the receiver at about waist height.

Bounce pass drill

On a wall, draw a line one metre off the ground. Draw a line 20cm below it. Stand away from the wall and bounce pass the ball to hit the wall between the lines.

One-handed bounce pass

When a defender's in your way, you can step to one side
and release the ball with one hand. This gives you valuable
extra reach to keep the pass away from the defender.

To complete this pass, step away from the defender with
your non-pivot foot and get low, before releasing the ball.
Drive the ball forward, thinking of it as skidding rather than
bouncing off the court surface.

STEP 1

STEP 2

Step-over bounce pass

Use this move when a defender
is in your face. Use your non-pivot
foot to step quickly to the side
and forward so that you step
around the defender. Your body
will then be between the defender
and the ball. Now you can make a
one-handed bounce pass.

Flip pass

The basics of the bounce pass can also be used to throw
the ball flat to the receiver without the bounce bit. This is
called a flip pass. Get your body low, but not quite as low
as you might for a bounce pass, and drive the ball with
plenty of arm and wrist power.

Flip tip

Flip passes are quite hard work for the new basketball player. Don't expect to be able to throw them over long distances. They are mostly useful at close range when space is tight. As with all passes, make them quickly once you know your receiver is ready.

From passer to receiver

A lot of failed, incomplete passes aren't down to the quality of the throw. They fail because the receiver is not expecting the ball, or because a defender intercepts the pass.

Don't make a pass unless you know your receiver is ready for one. During the cut and thrust of a game, it can be difficult to judge, but look for eye contact or a tiny signal and at the receivers' body position. If he or she seems to be squaring up to receive a pass from your direction, they're ready and waiting.

Pass drills

Every coach has a stack of passing drills and games in his playbook. Here are a couple of my faves, but there's nothing to stop you from inventing your own. Look to make crisp passes on target as the thrower. As the receiver, look to move well and catch cleanly.

Three v two

In an area ten-metre square, play three against two with no dribbling. Allow the player with the ball no more than five seconds to make a pass. For a real passing workout, shrink your playing area to eight metres square.

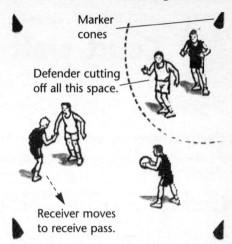

Marker cones

Defender cutting off all this space.

Receiver moves to receive pass.

One-handed bounce passes

These are one of the hardest throws. Get in some initial solo practice by making passes around a chair. When you're feeling more confident, try out the following hot drill with two friends.

In an area about 8m by 2.5m, take turns being 'Piggy-in-the-middle'. Use two- and one-handed bounce passes to get the ball to the receiver, but if the ball's intercepted or leaves the box, the last passer becomes 'Piggy'. Keep a tally of how many successful passes you complete in a row.

Pass notes checklist

Contact – the receiver must be expecting the pass.
Alert – be aware of changes in the situation.
Safety – only make the pass if it's safe.
Accuracy – pass accurately and quickly.

Court craft

Positions, please everyone

Players cover the whole court when they play, but are also given basic positions. Here are the playing positions shown by a team arranged in a common 2-1-2 formation of two guards, one centre and two forwards.

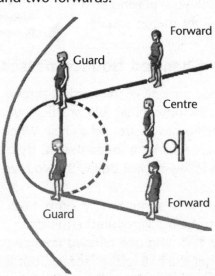

Forward

Guard

Centre

Forward

Guard

Guards – usually, but not always, the smallest players. The point guard who brings and directs the ball up into attack has to be a good dribbler and passer.

Forwards – versatile players, though one will be a good shooter. The other uses size and strength to play tough defence and goes for rebounding at both ends of the court.

Centre – often the tallest, who plays close to the basket in offense and defence. Must have good rebounding abilities both in attack and defence, shot blocking in defence and close shooting when attacking.

Size isn't everything

You don't have to be a two-metre-tall beanpole to be a great basketball player. The three-point shot and the need for guards means that smaller players with good ball skills are always in demand. There are and have been plenty of players well under 1.7m – Alton 'The Birdman' Byrd and Muggsy Bogues to name just two.

Violations and fouls

Basketball is a non-contact sport, but try telling that to a bumped and bruised forward after much rebounding. To stop things getting out of hand and to keep the game moving, there are a number of different infringements, called violations, personal fouls and technical fouls.

Violations

These are called by the referee, but do not count as fouls against a player. These include errors such as not taking a throw-in with feet behind the line, and travelling and kicking the ball. The ref's penalty: awarding possession to the opposing team.

Personal fouls

Illegal contact with an opponent (with or without the ball) is called a personal foul. Tripping, pushing, barging, holding or charging an opponent are all personal fouls.

Pushing

31

Charging   Holding   Illegal use of hands

If a fouled player was shooting, he or she is awarded one or more free throws depending on what happened to the shot. If it went in, it's counted and the shooter given one free throw to try to add a further point. If it missed, the shooter's awarded two or three free throws depending on the shot attempted.

If the player wasn't shooting, then the foul is recorded and possession simply passes to the fouled player's team.

Three free throws   Personal foul, no free throw

Technical and double fouls

Awarded for offensive language, threats or interfering with the taking of a sideline ball. Everyone on the team can be penalised with a technical foul. The result is two free throws to the opposition. If two opposing players foul each other at the same time, it is a double foul and there is a jump ball between the two players.

Technical foul

ACKNOWLEDGING A FOUL

When a foul has been called on you, raise your hand so that the scorer can see you. Failure to do so or disagreeing with the referee can get you into more trouble.

TEAM FOULS

Each team is allowed a maximum of seven fouls in each half. Any more results in two free throws to the opposition.

Double foul

OFF YOU GO...

A referee can disqualify a player, sending them out of the game, if their behaviour is bad. Even if not disqualified, building up five fouls (six in the NBA) means a player takes no further part. A sub can be used, but if there are no subs the team plays on with only four players.

Disqualifying foul

Starting play

Jump balls

All game periods, including overtime, start with a jump ball between two opposing players. If you're playing a game without any officials, the fairest way is to get one player (ideally a sub if you have one) to stand in, but make them close their eyes when they throw the ball up.

The ball cannot be touched until it has reached it's highest point. To win a jump ball, you need to jump as high as you can and to keep your eyes on the ball. If the ball hits the ground before either player gets a touch, it's re-taken.

Time your jump so that you are at a full stretch when your hand makes contact with the ball.

Look to tip or flick the ball back to one of your team-mates. You're allowed up to two touches.

Note where your team-mates are standing before the ball is thrown.
Avoid barging or fouling the opposition player or a foul will be given to you.

Held ball

If a ball goes loose on the court, it often happens that a player from each team will grab hold of the ball at the same time. This is called a held ball and the referee will arrange a jump ball between those two players. The jump ball will be taken from the place where the dispute occurred.

What's it to do with me?

Jump balls are often left to your tallest player so you could be forgiven for thinking, "I'm a shortie, I'm not interested in them." But if there's a double foul, a surprise stoppage when the ball is loose or a held ball, the referee may seek to re-start play with a jump ball which involves you. So, be on your guard!

Re-starting play – the sideline throw

The sideline throw is taken when the ball has gone out of play or for a violation. You can use any type of pass to throw-in. Foul throw-ins (where the ball is handed over to the opposition) only occur if both feet aren't behind the sideline when the throw is made and if the throw isn't taken within five seconds.

Throw-in tactics

Be alert. As you grab hold of the ball, look around for a free team-mate. Remember, time is tight so you have to be shot of that ball quickly.

If you're on court, look to fake and get free of your marker to receive the throw-in. Keep your eye on the player throwing-in as you make your move, and whatever you do, don't drag your heels!

Defenders look to crowd the space and make it hard for the player throwing-in.

A nice little mover

An enormous part of court
craft is getting free of a
defender and into a 'space'.
An attacker without the ball
can be called upon to
perform important tasks
like screening and creating
space for the player with
the ball. Just as likely,
though, an attacker should
be looking to safely receive
a ball.

When looking to receive, establish contact with the thrower
and move at speed. A good, balanced push off and fast
acceleration is vital. Keep your head up and stay alert.
Try to time your move to receive the pass when you're in
'space'. This will give you an enormous advantage over a
defender. You know exactly where you're heading; the
defender doesn't. The faster you move, the further away
you can get.

Space drill

Place two players eight
metres apart, each with
a ball. Stand four metres
back, behind a sideline
with another player acting
as your marker. Now, try
to receive a chest pass
from either of the players by
sprinting free of your marker,
but staying behind the line.

Speed drill

Nailed the space drill? Good. Now, try playing 2 v 1 in the centre circle with only five seconds allowed between passes – the defender doing the counting. Build that up to playing 3 v 2 in the key under the same rules.

Visit these drills again after you've learned about fakes.

Pace is ace

By now, you should appreciate the value of fast movement. Basketball relies on short, sharp sprints. Doing series sprints – a gentle jog followed by a ten-metre sprint and gentle jog, and finishing with a ten-metre sprint – will, if performed every day, help build up your speed.

Compass point sprint

Vary sprint training with this drill that also helps turning skills. Player B shouts out North, South, East or West, and player A sprints off a short distance. When player A returns to their starting point, player B calls out another compass point. Repeat ten times before switching roles.

So you've moved into space and got the ball...

Well done! Now, stop congratulating yourself and look for the next move. Whenever possible, adopt the triple-threat stance (see page 21).

If you're not facing the basket, pivot round to square up to it immediately. After all, if you're standing on the halfway line with your back to the basket, then it's only a double threat; there's absolutely no chance of you being able to shoot from that position.

Fake it

Fakes are pretend passes where the player cuts one way, only to actually make the play in another. They're incredibly useful in all situations, providing that you:

1 Make the fake convincing. Look like you really mean it.
2 Follow up the fake with a quick, decisive pass or move.

Simple fake move

STEP 1 ▶
You're being closely marked and need to get free. Plan which way you eventually want to head.

◀ STEP 2
To unbalance the defender drop your shoulder, turn your head and body and even take a couple of genuine-looking steps in the fake direction.

STEP 3 ▶
With the defender unbalanced and, hopefully committed in the direction of your fake move, turn sharply and sprint off.

Fake overhead to bounce pass

STEP 1

Look as though you're going to make an overhead throw. The defender will react by raising their arms and may even jump up to block the overhead pass they think is coming.

STEP 2

As the defender's arms raise, get down and make a speedy pass around the defender. If the defender is unbalanced, you may be able to make a two-handed chest pass, as shown.

The fake overhead to bounce pass can be done the other way round. Drive down and to the side to make a one-handed bounce pass. When the defender starts to follow you, get upright as quick as you can and make the overhead pass.

Pivot fake pass

Pivot round at speed, faking a chest or two-handed bounce pass. The defender will follow your moves or try to intercept what he thinks is the real pass. As the defender starts to move, pivot hard, usually back the opposite way and make your real pass to a different player.

Drills

Here are some more drills and games in which you can use your passes, cuts and fakes for movement.

Chest pass only

Go back to the three versus two box game on page 29. Keep the same box size, but only allow chest passes. This means that the thrower has to work hard to make successful passes. It's even tougher for the receivers. They've got to get free and into space. See how many completed passes you can string together. If the sequence is broken by the ball touching the ground or leaving the box, everyone switches positions.

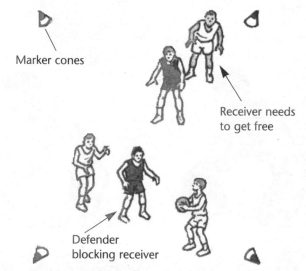

Marker cones

Receiver needs to get free

Defender blocking receiver

Triangle pass and move

For this drill, you and two friends need to form a triangle. Pass the ball in both directions around the triangle while moving at speed around the court. Try to maintain your positions in the triangle.

Dribbling and lay-ups

Your first dribble

Dribbling gives you real freedom to move around the court. But to say that dribbling is simply bouncing the ball with your hand is like saying that football is about kicking – there's more to it. So let's get cracking and start with a basic dribble.

Fingers, not the palm of the hand, push the ball down. Wrist flexes up and down to collect ball and then drive it down.

▶

STEP 1
Spread fingertips evenly around the ball. Bring your body slightly over the ball.

STEP 2
Bend your knees. Dribble the ball low, between knee and waist height. Keep the ball close to the body.

You can use both hands ...

Learning to dribble with only your stronger hand is a big mistake. It's like being one-footed in football – a serious disadvantage and one that a wily defender will quickly spot and exploit. Work especially hard on your weaker hand so that you can dribble equally confidently with both.

Get in some practice by dribbling along all the markings of a basketball court. Keep the ball bouncing on the line. This is a useful early exercise especially for your weaker hand.

... but not at the same time!

Two-handed dribbling – cool as it may look – is a violation. You and your team will be penalised by possession passing to the opposition with a sideline throw.

While we're talking rules, you should also know about the double dribble. You're allowed one dribble of any length you choose. But should you stop dribbling, touch the ball with both hands and start dribbling again, you've double dribbled. Penalty – the ball passes to the opposing team.

Rhythm and control

Don't slap at the ball – this isn't beach volleyball. Instead, let the ball rise into you hand, feel its surface on your fingers and then push down firmly. When dribbling think, 'pump the ball'. This may help you to build up a rhythm so that the ball reaches your fingers at regular intervals. Keep the ball close to you by keeping your elbow close to your body.

Head up

Bean bag is tossed between players.

Non-dribbling hand is ready to catch the bean bag. Keep your head up.

Now that your dribbling's coming along, you have to become comfortable with keeping your head up. If you're looking down at the ball, you're not seeing the action that's going down around you. Test yourself by playing this simple game with a friend. Each of you dribble a basketball with one hand, while throwing and catching a bean bag with the other hand. Sounds difficult, but it shouldn't be if your dribbling technique is right.

Protecting your dribble

Keeping the dribble low with the ball close to you is a good starting point in protecting the ball from a defender. In addition, try to keep yourself slightly angled to your opponent, so that the non-dribbling side of your body is between you and the defender.

Look to pivot away from a defender if he's tight on you. Unlike passing, you can pivot round off either foot to keep your body between the defender and the ball.

Practise, practise, practise

There's no secret or magic formula to dribbling other than to work on it as much as you can. Get comfortable with dribbling at different heights between just above the waist and just below the knee. Work on dribbling with both hands and get used to moving backwards, forwards and side-to-side, while keeping full control of the ball. You'll need all of these skills in a game.

One-on-one game

Play this in an area about 2m by 3m. One player tries to keep possession of the ball by dribbling and turning and shielding it. The defending player tries at every opportunity to pounce and take the ball without committing a foul.

Good control and quick turning protect the ball from the defender. Keep an eye on the defender so that you know what he or she is doing.

Dribbling tips

Temptation

As your dribbling skills improve, there's a great temptation to overuse them in a game. Remember, dribbling may be great fun, but you're on court to score points. The coolest dribble in the world, doesn't mean a thing if you end up losing the ball or gaining no advantage. Always keep your head up and look out for an opportunity to pass the ball, shoot it, or to make a drive to the basket or into an attacking position.

45

Disguising your dribble

Now's the time to look at the stealth aspects of dribbling. One of these is using simple changes of pace to outfox the defender. Moving from a gentle jog to a sharp sprint while keeping control of the ball can often surprise your marker and open up an attack. When combined with a switch of direction, a change of pace can be devastating.

Step fake

STEP 1 ▶

You receive the ball and start in the triple-threat position. Take your non-pivot foot and jab it down to one side or the other.

Pivot foot

◀ STEP 2

The defender is likely to move in the direction you have faked. As they move, straighten up.

STEP 3 ▶

With the defender committed to moving the wrong way, you should be able to dribble away in the opposite direction.

All kinds of dribbles

Get your basic dribble down so well that you can turn in all directions and maintain control. Then it's time to have some fast fun with crossovers and reverses.

Speed dribbling

From a basic dribble, lean your body forward and into the move. As you pick up speed, you'll naturally come out of the crouched position to become more upright. This means that the height of your dribble increases to just above your waist. To get the forward movement, you'll need to dribble the ball a little further away from your body. Protect the ball with your non-dribbling arm.

The speed dribble is fine when you're the player ahead in a fast break and when you're driving into the basket for a lay-up. In other situations when you want to move the ball fast, think 'pass'. Remember, the ball can travel faster than you. This means that swift, accurate passes cover more ground than even the fastest dribbling.

This is a good speed dribbling position. See how the non-handling arm protects the dribble.

Crossover dribble and fake

This is where the ball is bounced from one hand to the other with the ball moving from side to side. All good players seek to master this and many shift their body weight from side to side to help the dribble. One of the crossover dribble's most useful attributes is how it can be used to fake a dribble. Fake a dribble to one side of the defender, then switch hands and dribble round the defender on the other side.

◀ STEP 1
The dribble starts on one side. Keep the ball under careful control at all times. The shoulders are kept square to the direction of movement.

STEP 2 ▶
Keep the dribble low and your non-dribbling, receiving hand ready for the crossover move.

STEP 3 ▶
Bounce the ball quickly across to your receiving hand. Cushion its arrival with 'soft' hands and maintain the dribble.

STEP 4 ▶
You can stand a little taller after making the dribble move, or prepare yourself to make a crossover move back to the original hand.

The reverse dribble

This is a classic move when you're being tightly marked and dribbling. It's certainly one to look at and practise once your basic dribbling is going well.

◀ STEP 1

Plant your leading foot (the one opposite your dribbling hand) across and in front of your body. Shift your weight onto your front foot and pivot on it, turning your back towards your opponent.

STEP 2 ▶

Roll round your opponent using your pivot foot. Get your head in advance of your body movement so that you can check that's there space for you to dribble into.

◀ STEP 3

Use your other hand to make contact with the ball and head off in your new direction. As you do so, you should be protecting the ball with most of your body.

At the end of your dribble

You've got to end your dribble at some time with a pass or shot, so get yourself thinking about it in advance. Is your way clear for a drive to the basket? Is there a team-mate free and ready for a pass? If you stop dribbling and still have the ball, adopt the triple-threat position and get yourself facing the basket. Then, look to pass or shoot.

You can make a pass nearing the end of your dribble and before you've established a pivot foot by doing a push pass. It's like a one-handed bounce pass. Your last dribble movement is to push the ball away from you towards the receiver. It's fairly high-risk, but can open up a defence.

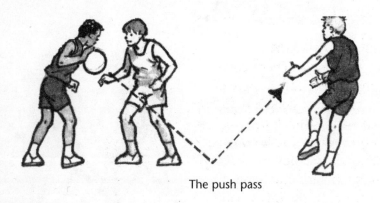

The push pass

Dribble drills

Box ball

Place two, three or more players in a marked out area. Each should have a ball. Players must dribble with their ball whilst trying to knock the ball out of an opponent's hand. Any player who loses control of their ball or dribbles or moves out of the box is eliminated. The winner is the last remaining dribbling player.

Dribble tag

In a marked out area, place three or more players each with a ball. The aim, while dribbling, is to tag each other whilst avoiding being tagged. If a player is tagged twice, loses control of their ball or steps out-of-bounds, they sit out for 30 seconds.

Relay races

Relays make good drills for speed dribbling, but you need at least two players in each team. Players dribble with one hand up the length of the court and once around a marker. They then dribble back to the start using the other hand. Each player does the same thing. The first team to finish is the winner.

Dribble slalom

Set up some chairs or cones in a line and dribble in between them. Look to keep a tight line round the obstacles. Get a friend to time you for a circuit going up and down the line, dribbling with one hand, then changing to the other hand.

To work on more side-to-side movement, stagger the cones, one metre to the left and right.

You can do this slalom as a team relay or as a personal challenge where you try to beat your best time over a number of sessions.

Lay-ups

Whether you perform a triple somersault before slam-dunking the ball or not, if your shot was inside the three point line in open play, it's worth two points. It, therefore, makes sense to learn the easiest way of scoring, and that my friends, is the lay-up. This shot on-the-move gets you as close to the hoop as possible before releasing the ball.

Basic overhand lay-up

Step made with same side foot as shooting hand.

Ball held in both hands.

Trailing leg 'hurdles' upwards.

Shooting-side foot planted.

STEP 1

You should be moving forward, feet off the ground, as you receive the ball. You're allowed two steps from this point. Make the first a long, bouncing stride.

STEP 2

As you land on your jumping foot, flex your knee and push hard off your jumping foot. Explode upwards looking for height not forward movement.

A lay-up occurs at the end of a dribble or on receiving a pass when you're moving towards the basket. Although there are fancy plays right in front of the basket, you will tend to make your standard lay-ups from either side. If you're coming in from the left side, your shooting hand is your left; from the right, your right hand shoots.

Target the corner of the square on the backboard.

Let your wrist follow through downwards after shot.

STEP 3
Stretch your body and raise both arms. As you extend your shooting arm fully, control the ball with the fingertips of your shooting hand.

STEP 4
With palm facing the backboard, push the ball to your target area. Not too hard or it will cannon off the backboard.

Talking lay-ups

*Rhythm is the top tip for lay-ups. Say to yourself, "**Collect-left-right-jump**" for a lay-up to the left side of the basket. Some players remind themselves of the movement by reciting, "**Collect-plant-stride-jump**".*

Cool cones

A good way to practise your lay-ups is to drive from the cone to perform a lay-up on one side. Collect the ball and dribble round the opposite cone. Drive to the basket from the other side.

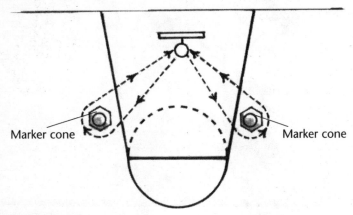

Marker cone   Marker cone

Group drill

Form two even teams. A player from one team makes a lay-up while a player from the other team makes the rebound and passes it back to the lay-up team. These players then switch teams, joining the back of the queue. Continue until everyone has had a few attempts at lay-ups and rebounds.

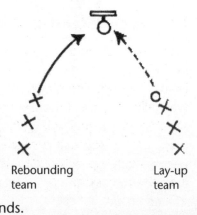

Rebounding team   Lay-up team

54

Drive to the hoop

So far, all of your
lay-ups have been
unchallenged,
however, that's
not what you'll
encounter in a game.

Start your dribble
from just inside the
attacking half.
Have a defender start
one or two paces
behind you to
simulate you getting
free from them.
Dribble hard and fast,
but under control to
the basket. As you approach, try to perform a lay-up.
The defender, for their part, will look to recover the lost
ground and then pressurise you into making a mistake or
not completing your lay-up. Do six of these, three from
each side, before switching places with the defender.

Give and defend drill

Add a twist to your lay-up drill by adding a player standing
in the key. He or she passes the ball to the player heading
in for a lay-up. The player in the key must time the pass
well, allowing the shooting player to collect the ball and
still perform a quality lay-up. An alternative is to use the
player in the key as a defender who looks to pressurise the
player laying-up without fouling or blocking the shooters'
way to the basket.

Shooting

Basketball is all about shooting and scoring baskets. Unlike other team sports, shooting isn't just the responsibility of a couple of forwards or attackers. Every player should be able to shoot. We've shown one way of scoring baskets – the lay-up – in the previous chapter. This chapter shows a number of other scoring shots and key principles that apply.

Shooting stance

Balance is very important for all shooting. Being balanced allows the parts of your body to move freely and with power and control. You need to stay balanced throughout the shot and follow through. The illustration (right) shows a balanced shooting stance.

Shooting stance – feet shoulder width apart, but with your shooting foot slightly forward. Toes pointing at the target. Shoulders are square to the flight of the ball and your head is centred over your feet.

Grip tip

Place your stronger hand on the back of the ball with your fingers spread evenly. Your thumb and little finger act as ball holders, while your middle three fingers do the pushing. Bring the ball up to the starting position so that it covers half of your face. Place your non-shooting hand on the lower front face of the ball to steady it.

Focus and your shooting line

You can choose whether to focus on the front, back or middle of the hoop, but always keep your eyes on the target before, during and after your shot. This helps you with your shooting line.

The ball should be in line with your shooting arm and leg throughout the shot. Elbow position is vital – it must remain directly under the ball during the shot and follow-through.

The shooting elbow is directly below the ball.

57

The set shot!

The set shot is not as spectacular as a slam dunk, but as it's the basis of the three-pointer, the jump shot and the free throw, not to mention a shot in its own right, you better know how to do it!

◀ **STEP 1**

Hold the ball with both hands. Your shooting hand is directly behind the ball, fingers spread and thumb just lightly touching the ball. Your non-shooting hand helps cradle the ball at the side. Keep your eyes focused on the basket.

STEP 2 ▶

Bend a little at the knees. Then, as you rise again, bring the ball up, too. Extend your back and shoulders upwards. Start to push your arm, wrist and fingers up and towards the basket.

STEP 3 ▶

Just before release, let go of the ball with your non-shooting hand. Your shooting arm continues pushing and extending. As you release the ball snap your wrist. Snapping your wrist gives the ball backspin, which will help the ball 'grip' the hoop. This 'grip' may be the difference between a ball sinking through the hoop and spooning out. As you snap your wrist, the ball should roll off your middle fingers.

◀ **STEP 4**

Follow-through with your arm and hand, and keep your eyes on the basket. Always try to make a mental note about how much force you used and your arm positions. Link this information to how the ball travelled.

Line and length

Get your shooting line right first, then work on the effort you need to get the right distance. This is really a trial and error period so be patient. Don't be disheartened by miss after miss. The very best players went through the same thing.

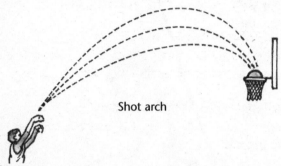

Shot arch

Getting the right length is not purely down to getting the "force" right, there's also the shot arch to contend with. This is the "arch" the ball travels in after you shoot it. Not enough arch will make it hard for the ball to fall through the basket. Too much and the ball will drop, short of the hoop. You can adjust the shot arch by adjusting how much your shooting forearm heads up rather than out.

Get into the groove

Good players spend hours working on the same moves to groove their shots. The idea is that your body gets used to the exact positioning and movement of its parts, so that it becomes a habit.

Start your shooting practice from close in, inside the key. Gradually work your way out to the edge of the key and beyond. Learn to shoot from all angles around the key. The 'Around the world in eight plays' game for jump shots (see page 66) can be used for set shot work-outs as well.

Shooting fault finder

Ideally, your coach will spot errors in your technique and help you correct them, but it's also good if you can be critical of your own shooting style. Below are solutions to some the most common shooting faults.

SHOOTING TOO FAR TO THE LEFT
Shooting elbow may be outside of the line, or your feet may be pointing to the left rather than at the target.

SHOOTING TOO FAR TO THE RIGHT
Shooting elbow may outside of the line, or your feet may be pointing to the right.

MISSING THE BASKET
Your non-shooting hand may be interfering with your shot. Try steadying the ball with your index finger, not the thumb, of your non-shooting hand.

HITTING THE FRONT OR BACK OF HOOP RIM
Your shot arch may be too low. Add more height to the shot by pushing your shooting forearm up more, reduce the forward thrust a little.

Free throws

Many fouls and infringements result in free throws taken from the free-throw line. A FIBA player taking the free throw has up to five seconds (10 seconds in the NBA) to take each shot from when the ball is handed to him. If the referee has blown for a personal foul, the player fouled must take the shot. If it was a technical foul, any member of the team can step up.

Other players stand outside the key waiting for the last free throw. On the last free throw they can move in, looking to make a rebound if the throw misses. A number of places are designated for attackers and defenders – they don't have to stand there, but if they want to, the other team must not stop them.

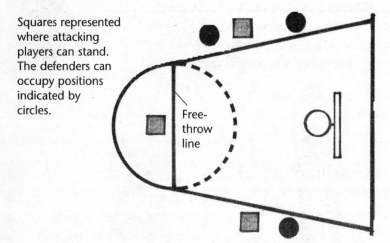

Squares represented where attacking players can stand. The defenders can occupy positions indicated by circles.

Free-throw line

Most players use a basic set shot, although some prefer a jump shot. It's up to you, but make sure your feet stay behind the free-throw line. Stay calm and don't snatch at the ball. If you have been awarded more than one free throw, learn from your first attempt so that you can nail that pesky second shot.

◀ STEP 1

Take some deep breaths and do your very best to relax. You may have been sprinting all over the court, but now is the time to calm down. Make sure you adopt a good initial shooting position, whether you use a jump or set shot, and ready yourself.

STEP 2 ▶

Don't be distracted by team-mates or the opposition players who are standing around the key. Maintain your balance and focus on the basket throughout the shot.

◀ STEP 3

Concentrate on a smooth, grooved action to your shot, remembering how you did it in practice. Two common faults are not following through completely and taking your eyes off the ball as it leaves your hand. Avoid these if you can.

63

Shot conditioning

This is about injecting some pressure into your free throw practices. A team of five line up with each player taking two free throws. If they make them both, the next player takes two. If they miss one, the whole team must do a forfeit – sit-ups or a quick sprint, for example. Triple the forfeit if both shots are missed. Harsh drill? Yes. Good practise? Definitely.

Jump shots

Much of the technique needed for a jump shot comes from the set shot (see pages 58-59). The jump shot is particularly handy in open play as it's hard for the defender to intercept when the ball starts its journey from height.

The start off position is similar to the set shot. Your head is up and your eyes on the target, but bend your knees a little deeper. The ball is held in both hands and your feet must point to the basket.

STEP 1 ▶

Place the foot on the side of your shooting hand slightly forward. Hold the ball with fingers of the shooting hand pointing upwards. Position your non-shooting hand to the side and slightly behind ball.

◀ **STEP 2**

Spring off with both feet, and lift the ball past your face to in front of your forehead. Keep your back vertical as your legs straighten. The shooting arm elbow stays directly under ball.

STEP 3 ▶

Extend your shooting arm fully. Ignore any defenders nearby and focus on the hoop. Release the ball upward – not outward – at top of the jump. Make sure your hands follow through.

Around the world in eight plays

Your coach may have a stack of jump shot drills and games, but you can't ignore this classic. Using seven points around the zone's edge players work their way around the key. At each point, they have to complete a successful jump shot, before moving onto the next point. With all seven completed, each player dribbles up to the other basket and sinks one final basket. If a number of you are playing, don't barge in, wait your turn and then shoot.

The crosses show five of the shooting positions around the key

The big three

If you've got a good set shot, jump shot and lay-up, you'll be a real threat to the opposing team. Fancy shots like hooks and turnaround jump shots can wait until you're shooting a high percentage of the big three in game situations.

Three-point shots and slam dunks

A successful shot from outside the three-point line is worth three, instead of two points. Three-pointers are hard to nail because you can lose control and line when injecting more power into the ball to cover the distance.

Vrrm, vrrm, more power

For three-pointer shots, you need to generate more power without losing your grooved shooting movement and shooting line. Try these two tips:

1 Your leg muscles are your body's power pack and using them to drive you up and forward creates more power without tensing your upper body.
2 Start the shot from a lower position. This gives you more arm power as you push the ball up.

A shot from behind the three-point line showing the drive from the legs. Although the player's drive from the legs and shooting arm position is good, she is making the common mistake of leaning too far forward and may lose her balance.

Creating space

Ideal three-point shot conditions include having lots of defender-free space around you. You may have to create some space for yourself. The fake drive forward and quick step back is one common technique.

Defender steps back.

◀ STEP 1

Start to drive past the three-point line, so that the defender is committed to moving backward.

Attacker quickly moves back.

Jump shot

▲ STEP 2

Step sharply back past the three-point line.

◀ STEP 3

Quickly take a jump shot while the defender is unable to block it.

Slam dunk

Let's get reasonable here. You've got to be a monster to be able to slam dunk the ball. A slam dunk is when the ball isn't thrown, but is carried towards and down into the basket. Only the very tallest and most agile basketball players will be able to manage this. Your coach, if he's working with adjustable height posts and is pleased with your training, may treat you by lowering the hoop so that you can slam dunk.

This player's coach has really lowered the basket for a bit of slam dunk madness. See how the player's hand is above the ball, pushing the ball down in to the basket.

6 Defending and rebounding

Sure, defence isn't as glamorous as shooting and scoring, but it's just as important. A player that isn't giving his or her all in defence is a player who'll soon be off the court and benched.

Let's start with the basic defensive stance. It's similar to the triple-threat stance, but often more crouched with your hands are up and out in a guarding position. You move by sliding your feet in the direction you want to go without altering your body stance.

As a defender, stay opposite your opponent's body with your back facing the basket as much as possible. Try to keep yourself between your opponent and the hoop they are attacking. This is especially important when your opponent has the ball and is dribbling.

Stay balanced so you can move in any direction.

Head up.

Foot closest to court centre should be leading.

Soft shoe shuffle

The shuffling, sliding movement is a lot like how a boxer moves around in the ring. Though it can feel odd, move on the balls, not the heels of your feet.

Play some simple one-on-one games where you, as defender, try to stay between the basket and the player with the ball. The attacker can use fakes and turns to try to dribble past you, but you must both play to the rules which means no pushing, charging or holding.

Direction of attack

The defender 'shuffles' around the court while continuing to face his or her opponent.

◀ *The defender steps back making it harder for their opponent to dribble past.*

◀ *The defender is always looking for an opportunity to intercept and knock the ball away or gain possession.*

71

Defending the attacker ...

... with the ball

As a defender, you're not there to make the attacker's life a picnic. You're there to make things as tough as possible. Harass the player to force a mistake, but do so without fouling or causing a violation.

Your arms are important defensive weapons. If the attacker is dribbling, one arm should be down low. Bring both arms up if it's shooting time, but be careful not to fall for a fake. In general, stand more upright the closer the play gets to the basket and keep alert for the attacker who is not protecting the ball – that's the time to strike and go for a steal.

When a player has stopped dribbling and established a pivot foot, he or she can't start dribbling again. That's the time when you should stand in closer.

... without the ball

With the pass thrown, the defender has swivelled round to make an interception.

First up, remember that your opponent is looking to receive the ball. You need to do everything you can to prevent him from doing so without incurring the ref's whistle. You're looking to stay between your man and the ball. You can do this by keeping your body facing the attacker, but swivelling your head back and forth so you can keep an eye on both the player and the ball. Your job is not be distracted from these two targets.

Turn and burn!

Whether they have the ball or not, if your marked player gets past you and is now closer to the ball and hoop than you, don't give up. If you react quickly, by turning and sprinting back into position you can often remedy the problem.

More defence tactics

When a coach says 'in his shorts', he means 'mark tight!'

Don't fall for fakes

As a defender you've got to try and spot the difference between an attacker's fake and a real move or play. It's tricky, but check out the movement of your opponent's hips for a brilliant clue as to their genuine direction.

It's a learning game

Throughout a game, learn about the player or players you mark. It doesn't take a tactical genius to figure out that an opponent can only dribble with one hand or that they're afraid of driving to the basket. With this sort of knowledge, you have a better idea of what they will do next.

The great thing about basketball is that everyone attacks AND defends. This means that what you learn in one area of the game, you can put to good use in the other. So, for example, knowing how to fake or make a certain offensive play can mean that you're able to spot an opponent starting such a move and can try to counter it.

Defending is for all players.

Defensive drills

Half-court games featuring equal numbers of attackers and
defenders (three, four or five a side) are brilliant practice.
So is marking out a ten-metre square box and playing
two-on-two. The defenders look to pressure the attackers
and prevent clean passes. Ten minutes of this with the pairs
switching roles is hard work, but great fun.

Defending checklist

Anticipation – think about what move the attacker is likely to
make next.
Commitment – keep defending no matter how tired you are.
Eye – keep it on the ball whenever possible.
Stay – on the basket side of the attacker.

Hands – always up and out.
Intelligence – learn how to counter the opposition's style of
attack.
Go – sideways by sliding your feet, not crossing your legs.
Hips – watch the attackers hips for signs of fakes.

And what does the checklist spell? **A-C-E-S H-I-G-H!**

Defending and rebounding

Team defence

Your team will most
likely play player-on-
player defence. But
that doesn't mean you
shouldn't know about
other defences.

Zone areas when
defending

Zonal or zone defence
is where each player is
responsible for an area
of the court. If an
opponent enters your
zone, you mark him
or her.

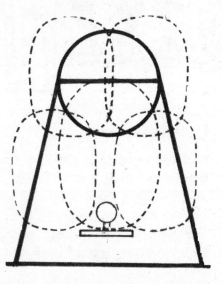

'Press' is short for
pressure defence and it
involves hounding the
player with the ball,
usually with a cordon of
players, to prevent a pass out or to gain possession. It
comes in a number of flavours, such as full-court and half-
court press, and is used mainly when time is running out.

Combination defence usually has a zone of three or four
players with any remaining defenders marking the
on-ball player.

Rebounds

Many shots are missed and bounce back off the hoop or
backboard. These are called rebounds and your team want
to collect them.

Basic rebounding jump

STEP 1
Shot comes in, rebounder gets into position. Head up and eyes on the ball, and weight on the balls of the feet.

STEP 2
Body springs up, arms fully extended to take the ball at the top of the jump.

STEP 3
Grip the ball with 'soft' hands and fingers spread. Gather the ball to your chest quickly.

STEP 4
As you come back down, bend your knees and spread your feet to land in a balanced stance.

What next?

As a defender, you'll be looking for an outlet pass (see page 81). As an attacker, you'll be thinking about a shot. On landing, really bend your knees and spring straight up again for a jump shot or lay-up. If a shot isn't on, look for a quick outlet pass to a team-mate.

Reading the rebound

Unlike the jump ball, which a ref throws straight up, a rebounding ball can come off the hoop or backboard in all sorts of directions. To become a good rebounder, you've got to be able to read the angles and predict where the ball is going to go. This skill comes only after lots of practice and experience. Get in some rebound reading with friends. Take turns throwing the ball off the backboard with different amounts of force, and then catching it.

Players in and around key put up shots from different angles and with varying force. Rebounder watches the shot, tries to 'read' it and attempts a clean rebound, before passing ball back out to the thrower and taking the next rebound.

Competitive rebounding

So far, so good, but you will rarely be rebounding a ball by yourself. You'll have company and it'll be of the opposing team's kind. Here's one drill that simulates this situation.

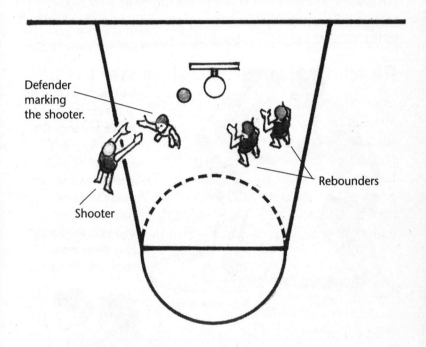

Defender marking the shooter.

Rebounders

Shooter

Two rebounders stand just inside the key. The shooter makes his shot from outside, marked by a defender. As the ball leaves his hands, the rebounders look to get into quality rebounding positions. The player who makes a clean rebound should immediately look to pass the ball back to the shooter who must get free of his or her marker. The other rebounder and the defender should look to stop the player with the ball. Score two points for a clean rebound and completed pass. Score one point if the pass is made only after the ball has hit the floor.

Blocking out

Blocking, or boxing, out means becoming a barrier to your opponent who is trying to rebound. Some contact is allowed, but pushing, barging or holding are fouls. Successful blocking out is about establishing a far better rebounding position than your opponent while the shot is in the air and before it rebounds.

Direction of pivot.

◀ **STEP 1**

As the shot goes up and players start to move towards the hoop. Step into the path of your opponent and get ready to pivot so that you face towards the basket and away from your opponent.

STEP 2 ▶

Make the pivot away from the attacker, taking care to avoid contact. Try to read the shot accurately for a potential rebound.

In a game, your team will be looking to box out all the attacking players. Three players positioned as shown in the illustration right, cover most rebounding possibilities.

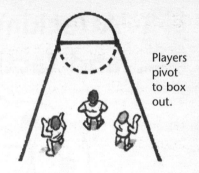

Players pivot to box out.

The outlet pass

Having made the rebound and with the ball firmly in your hands, tuck it up into your body. Using your body as a shield is really important in the rough and tumble under the basket. After you land, pass the ball as quickly as possible. This is called the outlet pass. A good outlet pass may start a fast break (see page 91), but whatever option you choose, make it safe so that your team keeps possession.

This is a safe outlet pass, wide and away from defenders.

It's a tough job

Rebounding is hard work that sometimes goes unthanked. Top rebounders are noticed and appreciated by coaches, regular spectators, in fact, anyone in the know. Sadly, that may not include your team-mates. But don't stop being fully-committed to rebounding just because they don't give you credit.

Attacking skills and tactics

Before we get into some classic moves and plays, there's a question of attacking philosophy and attitude on court. No player, however great, wins strings of matches all by themselves. Ask Michael Jordan. His team, the Chicago Bulls, never won the NBA Champs until other basketballing gods like Scottie Pippen joined the team.

Selfish players don't win matches. Basketball is always a team effort – every player must contribute well for a team to win. Your role and contribution may not be as flashy as others, but it's likely to be every bit as important. If you have the ball, always keep an eye out for a team-mate in a better position than yourself. If you haven't got the ball, search for a good position, in space, to receive it.

Draw and pass move

This standard fake-jump shot and pass-move sees one player sacrifice a shooting position to put a team-mate in for an easier lay-up shot.

Player 1's jump shot draws defender trying to block.

Player 1 releases a flick pass at the last moment.

Player 2 is in position to receive a pass and make a shot.

Don't jog, cut and run

Defenders think it's their birthday when the attacking team jog aimlessly around. Everyone understands that you can't sprint throughout an entire game, but when you do stand still or slow down, make sure it's part of a change of play.

Attacking skills and tactics

Where you move is as important as how you move. If it's a set play, great, you should know where to go. But if not, look to find space and places where the ball handler can reach you. Look to get into the danger areas for a defence – close to the basket and in good positions to shoot from. Worry the defence with your movement, but stay aware of what's happening in the game.

1 Don't block a team-mate's path and especially not the player with the ball.
2 Try not to crowd together. This makes life for the defence a lot easier.
3 Use the full width of the court where you can.
4 Be aware of a team-mate in difficulty. Move to allow an outlet pass.

Drawing a defender

Drawing a defender can create space for a team-mate. You've got to look like you really mean it and that it's all part of a move to convince a defender to follow you towards the basket to receive a return pass.

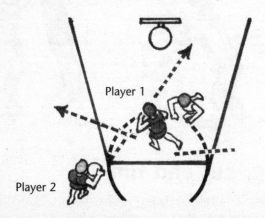

The attacker (player 1), arms out looking as though wanting the ball, cuts hard across defender. The defender is convinced and follows leaving a space for player 2 to drive to the basket.

Give and go

Like the one-two wall pass
in football, this is a simple
yet effective attacking
movement. The player
makes a pass, and cuts free
to receive a return pass.

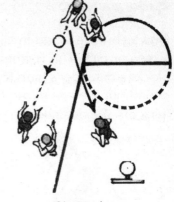

Give and go

Backdoor play

A move where the player
cuts back sharply towards
the basket. If successful, the
marker will be out of the
picture and the player ready
for a quality attacking pass.

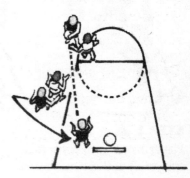

Backdoor play

Miss-pass

This is a three-player move.
Player 1 looks to pass to
player 2 who's racing
into position and starts to
check as the ball is thrown.
Defenders follow this
receiving player, but the
check is a fake – a miss-pass.
Player 3 collects the pass
and may shoot or pass to
player 2 who may be free
and close to the basket.

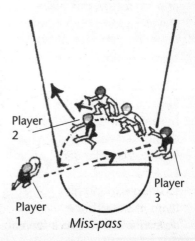

Miss-pass

85

Screening

One technique found in all offense playbooks is setting a screen or pick. This is when an attacker without the ball blocks a defender's path legally, allowing a team-mate with or without the ball to run free. It's often used to block or 'pick off' the defender marking your team-mate.

STEP 1 ▲
Player 1 passes to team-mate (player 2) and moves towards him. Player 2 collects ball and heads towards player 1. Player 1 plants his feet and faces the defender without touching him.

STEP 2 ▶
Player 1 tries to make himself as wide a barrier as possible without fouling the defender. Player 2 is now able to dribble round his team-mate with the defender less able to intervene.

Screening tips

Set your feet a little wider than shoulder width apart, and your arms in close. Set your screen early before the defender moves into you. Stay in the screening position until your team-mate has gone by.

Screening rules, OK

There are rules concerned with screening that you should know. You must be set and in position before the defender runs into you, otherwise you've committed a foul. Place yourself 30-50cm away from the defender, a little further if you're setting a screen behind a defender who cannot see you. Some light contact with the defender is allowed, but anything excessive like holding, shirt-tugging or pushing will be called a foul by the referee.

Don't diss da' netball

Apart from being a jerky thing to do, poking fun at netball, the closest sport to basketball, is wrong. Sure, there's no fancy hook shots and slam dunks, but with no dribbling allowed either, the passing and movement skills of netball is awesome. If you don't believe me, take on your school netball team at their game – you'll be sorry.

Try to play a game of basketball, full or half-court, with an even number of players, but with no dribbling allowed. In the key, you're allowed to perform lay-ups, but outside of the zone, just pass, pass, pass.

Attacking skills and tactics

Pick and roll

This is where the screen player rolls away from the defender after making the screen and often becomes free for a pass. After screening successfully, your foot closest to the hoop pivots and you roll away from the defender. This will often leave you closer to the basket than the defender. Look for a pass and scoring opportunity.

◀ **STEP 1**
Attacking team-mates attempt to perform a screen move that legally blocks the defender out.

STEP 2 ▶
As the player with the ball dribbles round, her team-mate rolls away from the defender.

◀ **STEP 3**
The player is now free to receive a pass from the dribbler as the defender is stuck behind her opponent.

88

Fast breaks

Exciting stuff this. If your team collect the ball from an interception or a rebound, they should look to make a fast break up the court. The opposition are still in attack mode and it'll take them time to set up their defence, too long if your fast break is fast and clever enough. You can make a fast break by a pacy dribble, quick passing, or a long, javelin-styled pass.

Have a break ... have a dribble

Good for interceptions and when there's a lot of free court ahead, you speed dribble as fast as you can whilst keeping control of the ball. Head down the middle of the court straight to the basket. Defenders will try to catch up, but you still may be able to drive to the basket for a lay-up.

Defender

Supporting attacker

Dribbler about to make pass

Supporting attackers, free for a pass, should be racing down court as soon as a fast break is on. The defender will be looking to slow you down or channel you into corner. If the defender catches you or blocks your way, look for an assist pass to a free attacker.

Fast pass masterclass

A fast break can be made with a series of slick passes between attacking players. The advantage is that the ball is switching position, making it a nightmare for defenders chasing back. The disadvantage is passing at speed isn't easy – the passes need to be a little ahead of the receiver.

Quick passing drill

Player 1

Player 2

Player 3

Defender

Three players, evenly spaced across the court, run up and down its length passing the ball quickly between each other. As the three get close to one of the baskets, players 1 or 3 should make a shot; player 2 rebounds. Make more of the drill by adding a defender. The defender tries to intercept the passes and challenges for the rebounds under the hoop. Keep swapping positions so that everyone has a turn in each attacking position and acts as defender.

Pilchard's Law (of fast breaks)

Griff Pilchard's a top guy, but a terrible ball player. Pilchard's Law is named after the way he plays. Pilchard's Law states that – **the quicker a poor player runs on a fast break, the slower his mind works.** Read on to see the law (and Griff) in action.

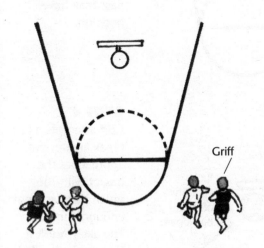

GRIFF 1

With the choice of the whole front court to run into, Griff has foolishly chosen not to get free of a covering defender. Griff is in no position to receive or pass.

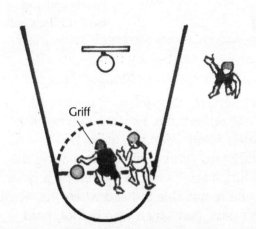

GRIFF 2

Griff receives the ball in the middle of a fast break, but is so brain-dead from his run up the court, he doesn't spot a team-mate free and in a great shooting position.

GRIFF 3

Griff dribbles at a blistering pace up the court straight into a corner where he's blocked off by a defender. If he looked up earlier a pass may have been on.

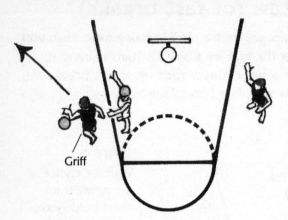

Griff

GRIFF 4

Griff attempts a fast break lay-up, but approaches the basket with too much pace and not enough control. The likely result is that the ball will slam off the backboard and back up the court.

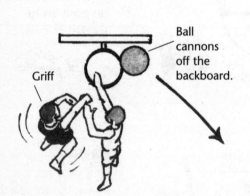

Ball cannons off the backboard.

Griff

Don't invoke Pilchard's Law when making a fast break. Although speed is important, clear-thinking is more so. A fast break is a terrific opportunity to score two low-risk points, and it hammers home your advantage by converting their attack into yours – effectively making the play a four-pointer. But, if you're not in rhythm for a drive to the basket, or if you're not able to head where you want to, PASS! If you can't pass, don't try a woolly shot, hold possession and wait for a regular offense to build.

Two-on-one

Mainly due to a fast break, but in other attacks as well, you can find yourself with a two-on-one situation. Lucky you.

Defender drawn to player with ball.

Simple bounce pass sets other attacker free.

Fancy moves

It wouldn't be fair not to show you some of the ace moves used by a good side in attacking. Only work on these slick moves after you've got your attacking/offense basics together first.

Javelin pass

In a fast break, if a player has broken free, you may be able to reach him by launching what's called a javelin or baseball pass.

Javelin pass

Move your weight from back foot to front foot, and whip your throwing arm forward. Use your non-throwing arm for balance. Follow through should point to the basket.

No-look pass and behind-the-back pass

These babies have a lot in common, and NBA players make them look so tempting and down-right easy. Yet, both are really hard to get right in a real match, so perhaps you should only use them in warm-ups and fun games.

For the no-look pass and behind-the-back pass, you need to know where your receiver is heading and he or she must have an idea of what move you're hatching up.

The no-look pass involves you looking in a different direction to the one in which the ball will travel.

In the behind-the-back pass, arch your body forward and slip the ball out behind you.

Trick pass game

In an eight-metre square box, play three-on-one, scoring a point for each no-look or behind-the-back pass completed, but losing two points for each fancy pass that fails. Any attacker who throws three incomplete trick passes, switches roles with the defender.

Hook shot

The hook shot is an advanced shot used in the key when you're unable to face the basket. To get the ball into the basket, it is 'hooked' or looped over your head. Your arm is well-extended and you should be standing side-on to the basket.

This is how to do a hook shot. Jump off the leg closest to basket. Carry the ball in an arc up and over your body. Your non-shooting hand holds the ball as along as possible, helping to control it and providing a protective screen. Release the ball with a wrist flick.

Brain over ball

The coach

YOU'VE GOT
SIX-PLAYERS
ON-COURT,
COACH!

The coach is your team's manager, the big chief, the boss! Unlike many sports, where the team captain calls the shots, the coach is the tactician and thinker.

During a game, the coach has a view of the whole game and can concentrate on what's happening to your team's shape and tactics. He or she can figure out what the opposition are up to and think of ways to counter them.

Because the coach is right by the sideline and there are lots of stoppages, his or her role is really hands-on. The coach decides on time-outs, signals the plays and switches the players on and off the sub's bench.

Time-out shout

When a time-out is called, catch your breath and take a drink, but LISTEN and WATCH your coach. He may signal a special play or get your team to adjust its playing style or formation. Many games are lost because the players don't listen or think they know best.

Substitutes

If you're playing flat-out, you're going to need breaks on the bench. Rolling substitutions allow frequent rests and changes of tactics, which can force the opposition into a re-think. You should be proud to make the ten on the team. There's certainly no disgrace in not making the starting five.

If your coach goes AWOL...

If your coach goes absent without leave, catches the flu or is kidnapped by a particularly sneaky opposition side, what will you and the team do without his or her knowledge, experience and sacred playbook? Well, listen up, because here's what you need to know.

Don't panic, don't get manic

Attacks can go crazy when a side is down by a stack of points in the second half, especially with just a few minutes left on the clock. This results in a lot of hasty, badly-thought out three-point attempts and snatched shots that don't allow your rebounders to get into position. Best thing to do is calm down! In basketball, you can claw back even a ten-point deficit in a couple of minutes if you play with a clear head.

Slow down!

Make sure you put a shot in within the 30 seconds, but remember, that's a heck of a long time. Don't be hurried into an immediate shot from a poor position. If your planned play doesn't come together and you still have the ball, don't get edgy. You should have time for another.

Use those subs and time-outs

A basketball game can quickly change. Keep the subs rolling and use time-outs to try to stop the rot and get your team focused. If there's an obvious problem, deal with it. Switch players around and discuss what can be done, but don't drone on or start arguing – time-outs last a minute, not forever.

Keep-it-simple checklist

1 In defence go for man-to-man marking.
2 In attack, remember the basics, such as getting rebounders into position.
3 Keep encouraging the players – arguing and abuse doesn't help your team-mates.
4 Play hard and sub often.

Missing something?

Your own court

I always dreamed of having my own court and badgered my Dad for years to concrete over the geraniums and erect a post and backboard. But unless you're Peter Posh or Renata Rich, it isn't going to happen. But, use your brain and it's just possible that you may be able to convince your folks, via hours of washing-up and good homework grades, to slap a backboard up. It'll need to be mounted on a brick wall that can take a masonry drill and away from windows.

Backboards and hoops can be bought from many stores. A cheaper alternative – almost as good – is a homemade one. Failing that, a backboard, chalked up on a wall by itself still allows you to practise many moves. Aim for the corners of the small square for side shots and the top line for shots from straight on.

Turn to page 102 for some more ways of practising your basketball skills without stepping onto a court.

Bad habits

You'll play a lot of fun games in the park and get all excited about the moves and attitudes of the pros. That's natural. But don't let bad habits creep into your game and spoil your play for proper basketball games. It's a matter of brain-over-ball, in other words, thinking before doing.

All mouth and foulers

It may look cool in basketball movies, but taunting and abusing other players is just plain dumb. The same applies to heavy contact, pushing and slapping players' hands as they pass or shoot. You may get away with it in the playground or park, but foul play and words are diseases – once they're part of how you play, they're hard to get rid of. Use foul language or rough tactics in a refereed game, and you'll be off quicker than you can say "White Men Can't Jump".

Dribbling forever

Dribbling your way up and down the court, evading your marker, is a great temptation. But in a real game, while you're in dribble dreamland the shot clock will be running down. And that's not all – you'll be ignoring chance after golden chance created by team-mates to put a score on the board.

Carrying the ball

This classic baddie occurs when a ball is bounced then held in the palm of the hand for what seems like an age before being bounced again. Your hand should remain on the upper part of the ball and while we're at it, the ball should never be dribbled over shoulder height.

Cheat!

Your friends may not be serious basketball players like you, so don't go around playing the expert with the rules and getting away with infringements like hanging in the key for an hour or disputing out-of-bounds calls. There's no point – you may have seen it in a movie and think it 'streetwise', but the truth is, it's cheating, plain and simple.

NO, REALLY, IT'S ALLOWED IN THE OFFICIAL RULES!

Tree power

If you have a tree in your garden that is well away from windows, you may be able to persuade a parent to fix a heavy-gauge wire hoop around the trunk. Shape the wire into a figure-of-eight, leaving the ends open so that they can be secured around the trunk. The solid ring becomes the hoop. Although there will be no board, it will still provide lots of opportunities for shooting practice.

No hoop, no worries

What do you do when you and your team turn up to the park to find all the courts taken? Well, there are several options. Practise the games and drills in this book that don't require a basket or mark out your own court with chalk, but add a one-metre wide circle in the key under where the basket would be. Play a standard game (only three seconds in the key and circle) with no defender allowed in the circle and one point scored each time an attacker receives the ball whilst standing in the 'basket' area.

Using a different court

If there's a five-a-side footie or rollerhockey court free, rest a target object on the crossbar of each goal and play a basketball game where no one is allowed in the D-shaped penalty area. Score five points if the object is knocked directly off the bar, and one point if a shot onto the crossbar shakes it off. You'll be surprised at the great game you'll have and how accurately you'll need to shoot to knock a target off the crossbar.

Hoop dreams

At all levels, from a simple playground two-on-two game right up to an Olympic final, basketball is a sport that is meant to be competitive. If you join a club or your school team, you'll want to test yourself and your side by playing competitive matches.

The Olympics

Since the 1936 Berlin games, basketball has been a popular men's Olympic sport. You may remember or heard about, the 'Dream Team' that included the cream of the NBA. True to form, they destroyed the opposition to win the Gold Medal at the 1992 Olympics.

Wheelchair basketball

Just as action-packed and as exciting as regular basketball, wheelchair basketball rules are a little different.

For example, a player's position is marked by the wheels of his or her chair and dribbling and travelling rules have been modified. Serious wheelchair players invest in specially-built, light and highly-manoeuverable wheelchairs.

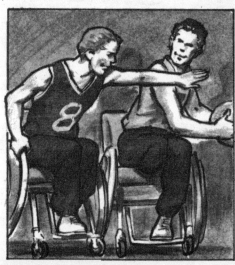

Mini-basketball

FIBA have established a whole new ball game for under-12 year olds. The new version of basketball is called mini-basketball. Mini-basketball is mixed, so the girls can really show the boys how the game should be played!

The court must be a scaled-down version of a full court. A good size is 22m by 12m.

Mini basketballs are smaller and lighter than full-size balls to make them easier to handle.

Pass receiver keeps an eye on the ball.

A defender in key.

All the regular skills of basketball – good passing movement, catching and shooting – are required.

Mini-basketball can be played half-court with three- or four-a-side teams. Here we show a mini-basketball game with five-a-side. All players in a team play an equal amount, often two full quarters of a game each. No one is left out to sit warming the benches. The whole point of mini-basketball is for everyone to have a great time!

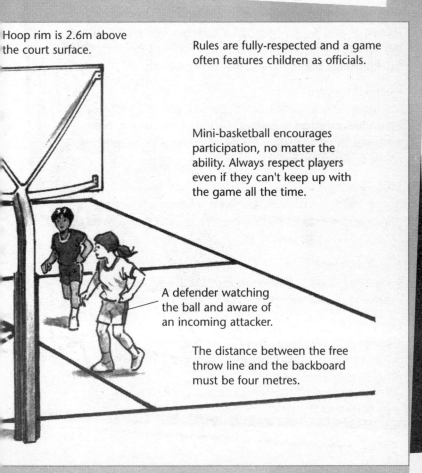

Hoop rim is 2.6m above the court surface.

Rules are fully-respected and a game often features children as officials.

Mini-basketball encourages participation, no matter the ability. Always respect players even if they can't keep up with the game all the time.

A defender watching the ball and aware of an incoming attacker.

The distance between the free throw line and the backboard must be four metres.

Basketball greats

Here are five of the biggest names ever to grace a basketball court and, I reckon, it's a pretty formidable line-up.

Wilt 'The Stilt' Chamberlain
An incredible physical force, the enormous Chamberlain was amazingly never fouled out. A brilliant shooter and passer of assists, he scored an incredible 100 points in one game! No one's ever got near that record or his average of 50.4 points a game for the whole of one season.

Michael Jordan
The man who averages more than 32 points a match is the man who turns more games than anyone. An astonishing athlete and ball-handler, Jordan defies gravity with his long range jumps and dunks.

Julius Erving
In the 1970s and 1980s, Dr. J was a brilliant attacking player and rebounder. He scored over 30,000 points in the NBA and was the hero of many of today's great players.

Magic Johnson
A great all-round player who loved to pass, but loved even more to win. Came with a smart brain for basketball, too.

Larry Bird
Like Magic Johnson, a terrific all-round player with a huge desire to win. Be it a three-pointer, a fast break or a sneaky pass, Bird was up for it.

The NBA

The United States' National Basketball Association (NBA) is basketball's big banana, the real deal, numero uno. The NBA's big pro team sides like the Chicago Bulls, the New York Knicks and the Seattle Supersonics draw huge crowds and attract top film stars and other celebs in a fight for court-side tickets.

If you watch any NBA action on television, you may find some aspects of the game confusing. There are a number of rule differences in the pro game that you won't find in FIBA – Federation Internationale De Basketball Amateurs – matches.

NBA players often make use of a jumping overhead throw.

Hoop dreams

So what are the differences? Well, to start the court is larger, being 28.5m by 15m, and the three-point line is one metre further away from the basket. The key lines are parallel with the sidelines.

Aside from court dimensions, the NBA and FIBA differ in these ways:

FIBA v NBA RULES

	FIBA	NBA
Game duration:	2 x 20 minute halves	4 x 12 minute quarters
Shot clock:	30 seconds	24 seconds
Time-outs allowed:	2/3 1st/2nd half	7 per game
Player foul limit:	5	6
Who calls time-out:	Coach only	Coach or player
Officials:	2	3

These basic rule differences don't explain away all the differences between an NBA and FIBA game. In the NBA, for example, a lot more physical contact is allowed and players are permitted an in-your-face-attitude. Though this 'aggressiveness' looks cool and makes for great spectating, don't even think about trying out NBA stunts under FIBA rules. Not only won't they work, you'll find yourself penalised with a technical foul for disrespecting an official or for baiting an opponent. You have been warmed!

The slightly rougher, more aggressive NBA game doesn't detract from the skill. Players in the NBA are the planet's best and it's every basketball player's dream to secure a starting spot in an NBA side.

NBA magic!

Want to see some outstanding plays and tricks of the NBA pros? Of course you do! Here's just a couple to whet your appetite. Don't expect to master these babies in your first or even your fifth season; these moves are tricky!

Driving dribble ... between the legs

Sounds impossible, and for all bar a few players like Grant Hill, it is. This move sees the player drive to the basket at high speed while foxing the defender by dribbling at speed through his legs. Not an easy stunt for the faint-hearted or short-legged player.

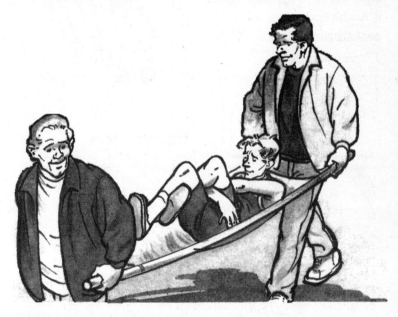

This player tried the driving dribble between the legs without proper practice. Look where it got him!

Sky hook

An old favourite of
such greats as Kareem
Abdul-Jabbar who scored
a mere 38,387 points in
his career, the sky hook is
a big, big, big hook shot
taken whilst in the air. It's
an immensely difficult shot
to get. How Kareem could
pull it off repeatedly in the
middle of a hectic game
with the fans screaming,
is nothing short of a
basketball miracle.

Reverse jam

When you see this behind
the back slam dunk in an
NBA or other top game, you
know it's showtime. Not
content with a regular slam
dunk, the player slams the
ball backwards into the
hoop by extending his arms
behind his head. The reverse
jam is one for the big men of
basketball like Shaquille
O'Neal or Patrick Ewing.

Fadeaway jump shot

This is Michael Jordan's trademark shot. He (and the other gifted pros who use this move) jumps up and away from the hoop and his marker. Because Michael creates so much hang-time in the air, he can easily pop his shot up over a defender's head and extended arms, and straight into the hoop. See this shot and it makes you go weak at the knees – it's so good!

Want to know more?

So you think you want to go for it, huh? You want to follow in the enormous size-16 footsteps of the best-ever players, play for a big team and lap up the glory. Well, first of all, there's just the small matter of improving your game 1000 per cent and then, and only then, there's the tiniest chance that you may make it. Still, as many great players have found, it's worth a try. On the other hand, perhaps you just want to brush-up on some basic skills so that you compete better at school or in the park. Either way, it's well worth considering joining a local basketball club.

More and more of these are springing up all over the country. Ask your games teacher or someone at your local sports or leisure centre, to recommend one. If there isn't a club near you, why not badger your games teacher to start an after-school club. If you can help rustle up enough keen players to make it worthwhile, even better.

As was mentioned many times in this book, much of basketball's training is great fun and feeds directly into your game. Practising with others is even more enjoyable and working on moves under the eye of a good coach will guarantee improvements.

Contacts

Here are a few key addresses of organisations that run basketball.

UNITED KINGDOM

English Mini-Basketball Association (EMBBA)
PO Box 22
Royston
Herts
SG8 5NB
Tel: 01223 207213

English Schools Basketball Association
Norman Waldron
44 Northleat Avenue
Paignton
Devon
TQ3 3UG

English Basketball Association
48 Bradford Road
Stanningley
Leeds
LS28 6DF
Tel: 0113 236 1166

Scottish Basketball Association
Caledonia House
South Gyle
Edinburgh
EH12 9DQ

Basketball Association of Wales
c/o 13 Hampton Court Rd
Penylan
Cardiff
CF3 7DH

Want to know more?

Irish Basketball Association
The National Basketball Arena
Tymon Park
Dublin 24
Eire
Tel: 01 459 0211

AUSTRALIA
Australian Basketball Federation
Level 1
19–23 Hollywood Avenue
Bondi Junction
NSW 2002
Australia

SOUTH AFRICA

Basketball South Africa
PO Box 57025
Springfield 2137
South Africa

Net Calls

UNITED KINGDOM
http://www.woods.demon.co.uk/
The homepage of the Britball website – an ace place dedicated to all aspects of British basketball. Full of news, reviews and features, this is the place to go for news of the Budweiser League, the Irish and Scottish leagues and lots more besides.

http://members.aol.com/engbball/
An interesting unofficial English basketball site but with plenty of links to other international sites as well.

www.basketballengland.org.uk
English Basketball Associations official web site.

www.basketballengland.net
The EBBA's own service provider, accessing E-mail and the world wide web and helping finance the initiatives and programmes of the EBBA. For info in the United Kingdom, you can call freephone: 0800–975–59–59.

AUSTRALIA
http://www.basketball.net.au/base.htm
The homepage of 'Nothing But Net' and it's true to its title, a dedicated site for basketball in Australia. News, views and tournament details are here along with fast links to the official Australian Basketball Federation site.

http://www.geocities.com/Colosseum/Sideline/1423/dunker.html
Although this site focusses on basketball in Queensland, it does have a good set of links to individual clubs and state organisations throughout Australia.

Want to know more?

UNITED STATES AND NBA
http://www.onhoops.com/
If you like American basketball, you'll want to check out this site. It's crammed with news and original features on all aspects of basketball in the United States and particularly, the NBA.

http://www.nba.com/
This is the official site of the NBA. It's written for the hardcore basketball follower with loads of team stats and profiles. Check out the video clips of the previous season's top ten plays. They're stunning.

http://www.coachesedge.com/
A novel website that offers loads of basketball coaching tips, many using computer animation. Although an American website, it's still of massive interest to players in other countries.

http://www.slamonline.com/
This is the online website for 'Slam' magazine and it is described as the only 'in your face' basketball website. It's certainly upfront and streetwise and has features on the big names in the NBA.

http://www.verticaljump.com/top100/html/reviews.html
Vertical Jump is a website for all sportspeople about how to jump higher. This is interesting to basketball players, but what's more, its list of basketball's top 100 websites is an easy way to get online to loads of basketball info.

http://www.bbhighway.com
Basketball Highway is a networking and information resource for basketball players and coaches. It's a slow-loading website, but that may be because it has links to several thousand other basketball sites all over the world. Don't give up, Basketball Highway is worth the wait.

Books

Rule Book
An important tome to have if you plan to play competition basketball. This full set of the latest rules is available from the English Basketball Association.

The Young Basketball Player
Chris Mullin
Dorling Kindersley
Good, large-page book written by a member of the United States 1992 Olympics Dream Team.

Better Basketball
Joe Williams
Sterling Publishing
Not the newest book in the world and hard to find, but it is still one of the best technique books around. It is full of really, really useful moves and skills. Check out your local library for a copy.

Basketball For Dummies
Richard "Digger" Phelps
IDG Books Worldwide
The Big Yellow series are better-known for computer books, but this excellent basketball volume, admittedly written for older teens and adults and with an American slant, is crammed with plays, stats and trivia.

Successful Sports: Basketball
David Marshall
Heinemann Books
A hardback book that's a useful and simple introduction to the world of basketball.

Play The Game: Basketball
David Titmuss
Good on the game's rules and the basics of organisation, this book also features some exciting shots of top players in action.

Want to know more?

Magazines

XXL Basketball Magazine

An excellent mag,complete with awesome action photos, XXL Basketball is available from most newsagents. It's a top read with tips from star players and lots of player profiles and interviews. Further details are available from:

Alliance International Media Ltd.

Unicorn House

3 Plough Yard

London EC2A 3LP

Tel: 0171 422 4200

Inside Stuff

A brilliant magazine, aimed at younger readers, full of NBA happenings. This and other American-based magazines can be purchased from 'Slam Dunk', a United Kingdom mail order supplier of basketball books, magazines and kit.

Contact 'Slam Dunk' at:

Unit 62, Smithbook Kilns

Cranleigh

Surrey GU6 8JJ

Tel: 01483 278989

Email: sales@slamdunk.co.uk

AUSTRALIA

One on One

PO Box 420

Carnegie, Victoria 3163

Tel: 03 9572 0911

Basketball NSW "Shootin' Hoops"

PO Box 198

Sydney Markets, NSW 2129

Tel: 02 9746 2969

Glossary

Air ball poor shot that doesn't touch the hoop or backboard.

Alley-oop big play for big players. One lobs the ball up to the basket so that a team-mate jumps, catches the ball in mid-air and dunks it.

Assist pass leading directly to a scoring shot.

Back court the end of the court a team are defending.

Back court violation when a team in their front court passes the ball back into their back court.

Bank shot shot off the backboard.

Benched slang for being substituted.

Blocking obstruction of an opposition player.

Boards slang for backboard. A great rebounder is often known as the 'Chairperson of the Boards'

Conversion a successful free throw shot.

Cripple an easy, unopposed shot at the basket, which is also known as a crip shot or a Snowbird.

Cut a fast movement made by an attacker without the ball to find space.

D short for defence.

Dead ball ball that's out of play or being used to take free throws.

Drive fast, aggressive dribble towards the basket.

Field goal any scoring shot other than free throws.

Front court the end of the court a team are attacking.

Full-court press pressure defence applied over the whole court.

Fumble accidental loss of control of the basketball.

Gunning the ball shooting too much when other team-mates are in better positions.

Half-court press pressure defence applied by a team in their back court.

Hang time the fly through the air before a high-jumping lay-up or slam dunk.

Glossary

Key the equivalent to football's penalty area.

O short for playing offence.

One-on-one single attacking player with the ball versus a single defender.

Outlet pass made by a defensive team on receiving the ball, usually to a player free near the sideline.

Overtime extra period of playing time to determine a winner if scores are drawn.

Sag term used for when a defender backs away from their opponents towards the basket they're defending.

Squaring-up turning to face the basket.

Steal winning the ball from an opponent fairly.

Strong side the side of the court where the attacking team have the ball.

Stuff another name for a dunk.

Switch where two defenders swap the attackers they were marking.

Tip-off start of the game.

Turnover losing possession without having taken a shot.

Violation infringements, like travelling, which are not fouls.

Weak side the side of the court opposite to where the attacking team have the ball.

Wing the area of the court between the sideline and the three-point line.

Index

A
attacking 82–95

B
balanced stance 17
    shooting 56
basketball 6
behind-the-back pass 94
Bird, Larry 106
blocking 80–81
bounce pass 24, 40
    one-handed 26, 29
    step-over 27
    two-handed 24–25
boxing 80–81

C
catching 17, 28
    faults 17
    stance 17
centre 30
Chamberlain, Wilt 106
charged time-out 12, 13
chest pass 20–21, 24
clock game 19
clothing 7–8
coach 96–98
combination defence 76
compass point sprint 38
court 4–5, 99, 102
    positions 4, 30
crossover dribble and fake 48

D
defending 70–82
double fouls 33
dribbling 14, 15, 42–55, 72,
    89, 100
drills 15
    bounce pass 25, 29
    chest pass 19, 23, 24, 41

defence 71, 75
    dribbling 44, 45, 50, 51
    fake moves 41
    jump shot 66
    lay-ups 54, 55
    overhead 24
    passing 17, 28, 29, 41, 90, 94
    pivoting 19
    rebounding 78, 79
    shooting 17
    space 37
    speed 38
    sprints 38
driving dribble between
    the legs 109

E
Erving, Julius 106
exercises 16–17

F
fadeaway jump shot 111
fake-jump-shot and pass-move 83
fake move 39, 68
    attacking 83
    defence 74
    overhead to bounce pass 40
    pivot 40
    step fake 46
fast breaks 89–95
FIBA 10,108
flip pass 28
    step-over 27
forwards 30
fouls 5, 72,
    disqualifying 33
    double 33
    personal 31–32, 62, 100
    team 33
    technical 33, 101
    throw-in 36

Index

free-throw 62

G
game clock 12
guards 30

H
held ball 35
history 3, 6
hook shot 85
hoop 6, 102

I
interference 15

J
javelin pass 93
Johnson, Magic 106
Jordan, Michael 106
jump ball 10, 11, 34, 35
jump shot 62, 64–66
jump stop 20

L
lay-ups 54–55

M
mini-basketball 104–105

N
Naismith, Dr. James 3, 6, 10
NBA 10, 11, 107–111
netball 87
no-look pass 94

O
officials 11, 12
Olympic sport 6, 103
one-on-one game 46
outlet pass 23, 81
out of bounds 12, 14
overhead pass 23, 24

P
passing 28, 29, 90, 93–94
playing time 11
pivot foot 19–20
    fake pass 40
press 76
pressure defence 76

R
rebounding jump 77
rebounds 76–81
referee 11–12
referee hand signals 10, 12–15,
    19, 31–33
reverse dribble 49
reverse jam 110
rules 4, 10–15, 19, 20, 43, 62,
    87, 108

S
scoring 15, 32
screening 37, 86–88
set shot 58–59
shooting 56–69, 95, 110, 111
sideline throw 36
sky hook 110
slam dunk 69
space, finding 37, 68
speed dribbling 47
step fake 46
step-over flip pass 27
stoppages 12
stride stop 20
substitutes 12, 13, 97

T
technical fouls 33
three-point shot 67–68
three v two 29
time-out 12, 97
trainers 7–9
travelling 14, 15, 20
triple-threat stance 21, 38

V
violations 12, 20, 31–32, 43, 72

W
wheelchair basketball 103

Z
zonal defence 76

ACTIVATORS

All you need to know

0 340 715162	Astronomy	£3.99	☐
0 340 715197	Ballet	£3.99	☐
0 340 736305	Basketball	£3.99	☐
0 340 715847	Birdwatching	£3.99	☐
0 340 715189	Cartooning	£3.99	☐
0 340 736496	Chess	£3.99	☐
0 340 715200	Computers Unlimited	£3.99	☐
0 340 736275	Cricket	£3.99	☐
0 340 715111	Cycling	£3.99	☐
0 340 715219	Drawing	£3.99	☐
0 340 736313	Film-making	£3.99	☐
0 340 736291	Fishing	£3.99	☐
0 340 715138	Football	£3.99	☐
0 340 736321	In-line Skating	£3.99	☐
0 340 715146	The Internet	£3.99	☐
0 340 736267	Memory Workout	£3.99	☐
0 340 715170	Riding	£3.99	☐
0 340 715235	Skateboarding	£3.99	☐
0 340 71512X	Swimming	£3.99	☐
0 340 73650X	Your Own Website	£3.99	☐

Turn the page to find out how to order these books

ORDER FORM

Books in the Activators series are available at your local bookshop, or can be ordered direct from the publisher. A complete list of titles is given on the previous page. Just tick the titles you would like and complete the details below. Prices and availability are subject to change without prior notice.

Please enclose a cheque or postal order made payable to Bookpoint Ltd, and send to: Hodder Children's Books, Cash Sales Dept, Bookpoint, 39 Milton Park, Abingdon, Oxon OX14 4TD. Email address: orders@bookpoint.co.uk.

If you would prefer to pay by credit card, our call centre team would be delighted to take your order by telephone. Our direct line is 01235 400414 (lines open 9.00 am – 6.00 pm, Monday to Saturday; 24-hour message answering service). Alternatively you can send a fax on 01235 400454.

Title .... First name .... Surname
....

Address ....

....

....

Daytime tel .... Postcode.....................................

If you would prefer to post a credit card order, please complete the following.

Please debit my Visa/Access/Diner's Card/American Express

																.			

(delete as applicable) card number:

Signature ....Expiry Date ....

If you would NOT like to receive further information on our products, please tick ☐ .